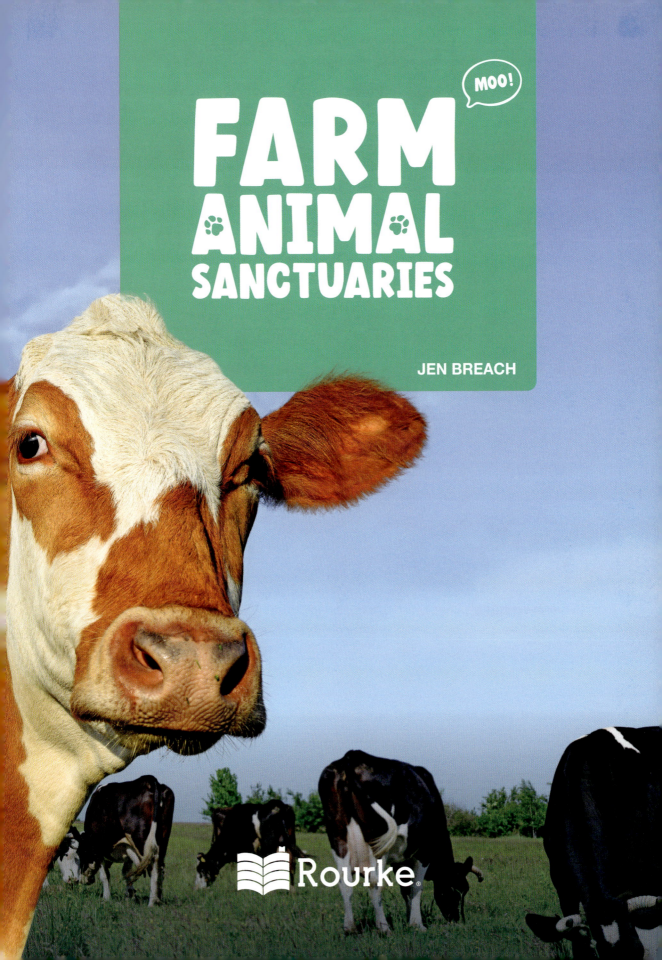

ROURKE'S SCHOOL to HOME CONNECTIONS
BEFORE AND DURING READING ACTIVITIES

Before Reading: *Building Background Knowledge and Vocabulary*

Building background knowledge can help children process new information and build upon what they already know. Before reading a book, it is important to tap into what children already know about the topic. This will help them develop their vocabulary and increase their reading comprehension.

Questions and Activities to Build Background Knowledge:

1. Look at the front cover of the book and read the title. What do you think this book will be about?
2. What do you already know about this topic?
3. Take a book walk and skim the pages. Look at the table of contents, photographs, captions, and bold words. Did these text features give you any information or predictions about what you will read in this book?

Vocabulary: *Vocabulary Is Key to Reading Comprehension*

Use the following directions to prompt a conversation about each word.
- Read the vocabulary words.
- What comes to mind when you see each word?
- What do you think each word means?

Vocabulary Words:
- abused
- domesticated
- donors
- humanely
- neglected
- rescued
- sanctuary
- volunteers

During Reading: *Reading for Meaning and Understanding*

To achieve deep comprehension of a book, children are encouraged to use close reading strategies. During reading, it is important to have children stop and make connections. These connections result in deeper analysis and understanding of a book.

 ### Close Reading a Text

During reading, have children stop and talk about the following:
- Any confusing parts
- Any unknown words
- Text to text, text to self, text to world connections
- The main idea in each chapter or heading

Encourage children to use context clues to determine the meaning of any unknown words. These strategies will help children learn to analyze the text more thoroughly as they read.

When you are finished reading this book, turn to the next-to-last page for **Text-Dependent Questions** and an **Extension Activity**.

TABLE OF CONTENTS

WHAT IS A SANCTUARY?..4

WHO LIVES HERE?..8

THE SANCTUARY LIFE...12

A FOREVER FAMILY...16

HEALING HANDS..18

GLOSSARY...22

INDEX..23

TEXT-DEPENDENT QUESTIONS...23

EXTENSION ACTIVITY...23

ABOUT THE AUTHOR...24

WHAT IS A SANCTUARY?

Many animals are raised to give us food, like eggs, milk, and meat.

Other animals carry heavy loads for us or run in races.

Some animals are our companions.

Sadly, sometimes these animals aren't taken care of properly.

Some might get **rescued** by a **sanctuary**.

RESCUE, SHELTER, OR SANCTUARY?

Animal rescues and shelters are different from animal sanctuaries. At a rescue or shelter, animals are looked after for a short time until they find a forever home. At a sanctuary, the animals stay—*this* is their forever home.

A sanctuary is a place where animals are treated **humanely**.

They have fresh air, good food, warm beds, and proper care. They don't have to do anything. They can live their lives peacefully.

WHO LIVES HERE?

Many sanctuaries care for one kind of animal in need.

A sanctuary in New Jersey cares for goats who need wheelchairs.

A sanctuary in Texas cares for blind donkeys.

A sanctuary in Wisconsin cares for dogs and cats who are "unadoptable." Most are old or have special needs.

Other sanctuaries care for many kinds of **domesticated** animals.

One sanctuary like this is in New York state. It cares for more than 1,200 chickens, ducks, geese, cows, sheep, goats, pigs, horses, donkeys . . . and one cat!

Most animals who come to a sanctuary have been **neglected** or **abused**. Sanctuaries help to heal emotional and physical wounds.

THE SANCTUARY LIFE

At dawn, animals wake up in cozy straw beds. Rise and shine! It's breakfast time!

Afterwards, pigs will snuffle in wooded areas or wallow in mud. Chickens will scratch and peck up juicy worms. Sheep will graze in wide-open fields.

Cows will have a good scratch on a post or nudge a ball around with their head. Goats will climb and leap and wag their tails happily.

At dusk, it's dinnertime. Then, it is time for bed. Another peaceful day at the sanctuary is done.

On hot summer days, there are cool treats. Animals might lick vegetables frozen in ice, play in sprinklers, or nap in the sunshine.

On cold winter days, they might not even leave their warm barn. They might doze in deep, cozy hay and enjoy a hug or a belly rub.

At sanctuaries, animals are never kept in kennels or cages. They have room to stretch, roam, and play freely.

A FOREVER FAMILY

Animals at sanctuaries often form close friendships. They might graze or doze together. They might groom each other. These friendships help the animals heal.

Sometimes an animal might "adopt" another animal. Dogs and cats often raise kittens, puppies, or fluffy yellow chicks that aren't their own.

HEALING HANDS

People who run sanctuaries believe that if humans can *hurt* animals, then humans can *help* them too. But running a sanctuary is hard work! They need lots of support.

Volunteers might repair buildings or fences. **Donors** might give money for food, bedding, or medicine for the animals.

MEATLESS MEALS

A great way to support sanctuaries is to eat less meat and more plants!

How can you help?

You can volunteer at a sanctuary. You might be able to sponsor an animal too. Who would you choose to sponsor?

TASTY TREATS

Some sanctuaries welcome seasonal gifts, like leftover pumpkins, unsellable apples, or post-holiday trees. The animals love to eat them!

You can visit a sanctuary to learn about it. You won't see animals sitting in cages or performing tricks. You will see happy, carefree animals doing just what they love to do—be animals!

GLOSSARY

abused (uh-BYOOZ-d) having been treated cruelly

domesticated (duh-MES-ti-kay-ted) tame

donors (DOH-nurz) people who give something, usually to an organization or charity

humanely (hyoo-MANE-lee) kindly and respectfully

neglected (ni-GLEK-ted) not taken care of

rescued (RES-kyoo-d) saved from danger

sanctuary (SANGK-choo-er-ee) a place where animals are protected

volunteers (vah-luhn-TEERZ) people who work without being paid

INDEX

companions 4

donkeys 9, 10

food 4, 7, 19

friendships 16

goats 8, 10, 13

heal 11, 16

humans 18

shelter 6

TEXT-DEPENDENT QUESTIONS

1. How is a sanctuary different from a rescue?
2. Why might an animal end up in a sanctuary?
3. Why do you think animals in a sanctuary form friendships?
4. Name four things that sanctuaries provide for their animals.
5. What are two things a person could do to support a sanctuary?

EXTENSION ACTIVITY

Imagine that you are going to visit a farm animal sanctuary. Write a story about your visit. What animals might you see? What might you do there? Who might you meet? Draw pictures to go with your story.

Share your story with a friend or family member.

ABOUT THE AUTHOR

Jen Breach (they/them) is a queer, nonbinary writer living in a tiny row home in South Philly. Jen grew up next door to a humane cattle farm in rural Australia and raised a rescued duck as a companion animal. Her name was Darren and she was the best.

© 2025 Rourke Educational Media

All rights reserved. No part of this book may be reproduced or utilized in any form or by any means, electronic or mechanical including photocopying, recording, or by any information storage and retrieval system without permission in writing from the publisher.

www.rourkebooks.com

PHOTO CREDITS: Cover, Page 1: ©Shutterstock.com/smereka; Cover, Pages 1, 3, 4, 5, 7, 8, 9, 10, 12, 13,14,15, 16, 17, 18, 19, 20, 21, 22, 23, 24: ©Getty Images/Anna Bliokh; Page 4: ©Getty Images/Smederevac; Page 5: ©Getty Images/SureshMenon; Pages 6-7: ©Getty Images/undefined undefined; Page 7: ©Shutterstock.com/Nelida Zubia; Pages 8-9: ©Getty Images/Guillem de Balanzo; Pages 10-11: ©Getty Images/SilvaPinto1985; Page 12: ©Shutterstock.com/Dusan Petkovic; Page 13: ©Shutterstock.com/Russ Gallagher; Page 14: ©Shutterstock.com/dayandnightcollective; Page 15: ©Getty Images/vikarus; Page 16: ©Getty Images/aydinmutlu; Page 17: ©Shutterstock.com/Tracey Helmboldt; Page 18: ©Getty Images/vgajic; Page 19: ©Getty Images/PeopleImages; Page 20: ©Getty Images/heebyj; Page 20: ©Shutterstock.com/Denis Tabler; Page 20: ©Shutterstock.com/Kravatsiz Adam; Page 20: ©Getty Images/Peter Vahlersvik; Page 21: ©Shutterstock.com/BMJ

Edited by: Catherine Malaski
Cover, interior layout, and interior illustrations by: Max Porter

Library of Congress PCN Data

Farm Animal Sanctuaries / Jen Breach
(Animal Sanctuaries)
ISBN 978-1-73165-805-0 (hard cover)(alk. paper)
ISBN 978-1-73165-811-1 (soft cover)
ISBN 978-1-73165-817-3 (e-book)
ISBN 978-1-73165-823-4 (e-pub)
Library of Congress Control Number: 2024903471

Rourke Educational Media
Printed in the United States of America
01-2222411937